This book was produced by the School of Journalism

SIU Southern Illinois University

CARBONDALE

www.siu.edu

Just hours after a deadly tornado descended into Harrisburg, Ill. on Feb. 29, 2012, reporters and photographers from the Daily Egyptian arrived on the scene. The next day, their stories and pictures reported the story on the front page of the Chicago Tribune.

When the early rush of stories ended and national news organizations moved on, Journalist-in-Residence William Recktenwald reminded us that the story wasn't over. It was beginning. While traveling through the town every day he saw the residents picking themselves up with remarkable determination. This book tells that story.

Students from the Daily Egyptian's spring staff wrote the story and shot many of the images, supplemented by other student photojournalists. Students Sharon Wittke, Lauren Leone and Steve Matzker worked into the summer. Recktenwald led the effort. Chancellor Rita Cheng heard about the project and advanced money for printing. Photography professors Mark Dolan and Phil Greer counseled students on the images and design.

Public service is the highest form of journalism. Journalists are not detached from their communities, nor are universities. Journalists are the storytellers of their communities. This tragic event provided an opportunity for our students to see firsthand what they only read about in the classroom. But this book isn't about us. It is about the community in and around Harrisburg and Ridgway. This is the story of how our neighbors picked themselves up, buried their dead and rebuilt their lives.

Bill Freivogel
Director, School of Journalism

Proceeds from the sale of this book will be donated to area organizations aiding in the rebuilding efforts.

Introduction

OFFICE OF THE CHANCELLOR   618/453-2341
ANTHONY HALL 116   618/453-5362 FAX
MAIL CODE 4304
1265 LINCOLN DRIVE
CARBONDALE, ILLINOIS 62901

chancellor.siuc.edu

Dear Reader:

Words cannot adequately describe the terror and tragedy that struck our friends and neighbors in Harrisburg and Ridgway at 4:56 a.m. on February 29, 2012. The compelling images that follow, however, speak volumes about the magnitude of this disaster.

As they chronicled the devastation, our photojournalism students and faculty also captured the essence of who we are in Southern Illinois. Within minutes of the EF4 tornado passing, first responders and many other good Samaritans rushed to the stricken communities in an effort to save lives and tend to the injured.

In the hours, days and weeks that followed, hundreds of people shared their time and treasure to assist with the recovery, including students, faculty and staff from SIU Carbondale. They contributed in many ways -- donating time and effort, food, supplies, and money -- to help so many who had lost so much.

Some who volunteered -- along with participants in this book project -- perhaps came face-to-face with tragedy and loss of life for the first time. They learned valuable lessons about compassion and reaching out to those in need. And they learned about the incredible determination of the residents of Harrisburg and Ridgway.

We are pleased to donate the proceeds from the sale of this book, produced by our School of Journalism, to the ongoing recovery effort. The courage and resiliency of the residents of these communities, and the spirit of generosity shown by so many, will forever serve as inspiration to all of us.

Sincerely,

Rita Cheng

Rita Cheng
Chancellor
SIU Carbondale

Foreword

SHEILA SIMON
LIEUTENANT GOVERNOR
STATE OF ILLINOIS

This book is all about community.

On February 29, 2012, a tornado struck Southeastern Illinois. In short order it left its mark of destruction. But what the tornado could not tear apart is our sense of community in Southern Illinois.

I had the opportunity to go to Harrisburg on the day of the tornado. Law enforcement officers and health care workers were executing well planned mutual support agreements. Squad cars and ambulances from across the region were in Saline and Gallatin Counties.

But it wasn't just the organized and planned help that responded.

People from throughout the region responded, using their skills and talents where they knew there would be need. Miki Pavelonis, who lives in Harrisburg, had the roof torn off of her house, but quickly made sure that all her neighbors were safe. Tammi Shultz, a lawyer from Jackson County, put down her legal work, grabbed her chainsaw, and headed for Harrisburg. Friends made room for the newly homeless to live with them temporarily, and church basements teemed with volunteers offering everything from bologna sandwiches to cleaning supplies.

The community continued beyond that first frightening day. Organized efforts by the Red Cross and the state emergency management agency were comprehensive and orchestrated. And help came from unexpected sources as well, like a long list of local musicians who donated performances to help raise money.

This book is one of those examples of community. Photojournalism students from SIU used their skills to record a storm that had to be seen to be fully appreciated. And the proceeds of this book, produced by the School of Journalism, will go to support survivors who continue the process of rebuilding.

Thanks to the relatives, friends and strangers who came together to secure, repair and rebuild. And thanks to the photographers who have done elegant work in preserving these scenes. It's good to be a part of such a community.

Sincerely,

Sheila Simon
Lt. Governor of Illinois

IDOT
District 9 Headquarters
Carbondale, IL 62903
Phone: (618) 529-6452
Fax: (618) 529-6455

214 State House
Springfield, IL 62706
Phone: (217) 558-3085
Fax: (217) 558-3094
TTY : 1-800-563-7110

JRTC, 15-200
Chicago, IL 60601
Phone: (312) 814-5240
Fax: (312) 814-5228

Devastation before dawn

You could hear a pin drop

-Bill Summers
Harrisburg Fire Chief

Story by Sharon Wittke and Sarah Schneider

Before dawn on Leap Day 2012, an eerie stillness fell on Harrisburg, Ill.

"The wind quit blowing and it turned deathly quiet," recalled Fire Chief Bill Summers, who was standing outside his car on Highway 13 watching for a tornado. "You could hear a pin drop."

Mayor Eric Gregg heard the eerie silence too as he shoved heirlooms under the bed.

Moments later, at 4:56 a.m., an EF-4 tornado, unseen in a veil of rain, descended on the small, sleeping town killing six and injuring 100, two so badly that they died later.

And then the tornado was gone.

"It was here and gone in a flash," said Joy Emery, a longtime resident.

Kim Dunn, who worked at the hospital, hurried home to locate her family, but debris blocked her car.

She got out to walk.

"The really weird part was hearing people yell for help everywhere and you couldn't see anybody," she said.

Once the sun rose, the damage was

Automobiles were strewn about like toys as the EF-4 tornado ripped through the Harrisburg area. | ERIC GINNARD

worse than imagined. More than 200 homes and about 25 businesses were destroyed or heavily damaged. A strip mall on Highway 45 was completely leveled.

But even before sunrise, Harrisburg had begun to pick itself up.

Diana Turner climbed out of a pile of rubble after her trailer home blew away. She never had to call for help. "Everybody just showed up," she said.

As Mayor Gregg put it, "People in this community did not run from this devastation, they ran to it. And the reason they ran to it was to help others."

SIREN SOUNDS IN A SLEEPING TOWN

Rick Mallady, Harrisburg's emergency management agency coordinator and a city firefighter, had been tracking the massive storm system on his home computer as it made its way across the Midwest.

Kelly Hooper, an incident meteorologist for the National Weather Service in Paducah, Ky., had kept in close touch with emergency officials.

People walk through the carnage at the Gaskins City subdivision on the southeast side of Harrisburg. | LYNNETTE OOSTMEYER

"We knew a day or so ahead of time that environmental conditions were favorable for major tornadic activity," he said.

At about 4 a.m. Mallady left his house and joined Chief Summers and the two fire fighters on duty, Jim Jones and John Quisenberry, at the fire station.

Summers had heard from weather spotters in Goreville and Creal Springs, southwest of Harrisburg, that a dangerous storm was approaching.

Shortly after 4:30 a.m., Mallady directed Quisenberry to activate the four outdoor sirens, alerting the city's residents of the rapidly approaching tornado.

Then Mallady, Summers and a third firefighter, Brandon Culkin, jumped in their vehicles and drove off in different directions to watch for the tornado. They never saw it.

Summers positioned himself on Highway 13 and looked westward toward Marion. He was standing next to his car studying the churning sky when he noticed a difference in the quality of the air, a "deathly quiet."

"I couldn't get to the car fast enough."

Meanwhile, Tracy Felty, a lieutenant in the Saline County Sheriff's Department and director of the Saline County 9-1-1 center, was driving on Highway 45 northeast of Stonefort when he saw flashes of light in the sky as the tornado hit transformers north of Carrier Mills at 4:51 a.m.

Five minutes later, the tornado smashed into the south side of Harrisburg seven miles to the northeast, destroying a section of Dorrisville before it skipped across Highway 45 and began its deadly attack on the Gaskins City neighborhood.

Within twenty minutes, the tornado's 185-mph winds left a 275-yard wide path of destruction 26.5 miles long. | **ALEXA ROGALS**

Several minutes later, it left Saline County and crashed into the small Gallatin County village of Ridgway at 5:10 a.m., destroying the town's century-old Catholic Church and damaging 140 homes and businesses. Twelve were injured, one critically.

It took less than 20 minutes for the 275-yard-wide tornado, whose wind speed reached 180 mph, to travel a 26.5 mile path from Carrier Mills to Ridgway.

Felty reached Harrisburg minutes after the tornado touched down and thought it looked "like a bomb went off."

"I saw a building sitting in the middle of 45," Felty said. "I tried to figure it out, then I realized it was Energy Mart."

As he scanned the scene, he saw debris from the Golden Circle and Dream Baskets buildings strewn over the highway. The Golden Circle is a large nutrition center for seniors. At noon it would have had 100 people eating lunch.

"Then I thought, 'Where's the Lutheran Church?' The brick church was gone," Felty said.

Chief Summers returned to town to see that "the power lines looked like spaghetti."

Mayor Gregg had gone to bed knowing there was a possibility of severe weather. But he thought, "It has always gone over us and around us but never hit us."

The sirens were still blaring
and the city radio was going of

Gregg awoke before the storm hit and sent his wife and youngest son to the neighbor's house as he collected family heirlooms. Then silence fell as the rain stopped.

"The sirens were still blaring and the city radio was going off and we could hear officers saying it had touched down and there was devastation," he said. "It was the most horrible feeling you could possibly have because of the looming danger that was upon us. It really became our worst nightmare."

OPERATION BLESSING

Ron Patterson heard cries for help as he emerged from his own damaged house in Dorrisville, on the southwest side of Harrisburg. He grabbed a flashlight and walked toward the cries in the inky darkness.

His neighbor, Utha Angelly, and her friend, Jane Buti, who was visiting from Terre Haute, Ind., were trapped beneath Angelly's house.

"My flashlight went dead, so I told her to keep hollering," Patterson said. "I couldn't see anything, but I finally found Utha and her friend, and carried them out and back to our house."

Neither woman had serious injuries.

About the same time, Roy Mauney was searching through debris in the Gaskins City subdivision for his parents.

He had been getting ready for work when one of his neighbors burst into his house and told him he needed to get to his parents right away.

Mauney made his way to Texas Street and saw that his parents' house had been torn from its foundation and flung into another dwelling nearly 100 feet away.

"It was dark and windy. There were gas leaks and power lines down everywhere," Mauney said.

Utha Angelly, of Harrisburg, cleans up debris around her house. | DANIELLE MCGREW

My flashlight went dead
so I told her to keep hollering

"We could hear them – we could hear my mother calling," he said. "I kind of dropped to the ground and began looking for them."

He found his parents Rebecca and Blaine Mauney lying in their bathtub in a three-foot hole, both suffering from serious injuries. Rebecca recovered, but Blaine died May 31.

At the Harrisburg Medical Center, Kim Dunn had been pulling into work when she heard tornado sirens. She called her husband but couldn't reach him. Then she noticed a wall missing from the hospital. But she never spotted the tornado.

She set off to find her family but could not drive down a nearby street blocked by debris. So she parked, grabbed a flashlight and tried to walk home, hearing people crying out for help but not seeing them.

Dunn helped one neighbor to safety before continuing down the road to find her husband, son and mother unharmed. Their house was a mess. Half the carport was flattened, parts of the roof were missing and ceiling tiles had fallen inside the house.

Nearby, jars of spaghetti sauce, salsa and pie filling – most of them unbroken - lay scattered along the road. Clothing and sheets rustled in smashed windows and pink insulation covered trees. Some homes looked like dollhouses with walls ripped off leaving the contents visible. Family photos, clothing, dishes – everything that makes a home – were scattered to the winds.

When Diana Turner's mobile home was destroyed, she found herself in a pile of debris. The storm had thrown her husband, Charles, about 50 feet away and dumped a cabinet on top of him.

But Diana Turner didn't even have to call for help. Bonnie Mahan, a Harrisburg Lake resident and family friend, had heard what happened and drove there immediately. Last year the Turners had helped her when the area around her home was flooded. Charles was taken to the hospital but released shortly after with minor scrapes and bruises.

On Roosevelt Street, Greg Thomas was just shutting his basement door when his wife, Lisa, pulled him down the stairs. Moments later, the roof blew off.

As soon as the winds died down, Thomas grabbed his generator and took it to his neighbor's house.

"It was great that he thought to bring over the generator," said Wayne Edwards, whose grandson uses a ventilator.

Allan Ninness, director of the Saline County Emergency Management Agency, said 3,000 volunteers helped during the three weeks after the storm.

When 20 coal miners trained in underground search-and-rescue operations from Willow Grove and other nearby Peabody Energy Company mines arrived, suited up and ready to work, Chief Summers said he felt an overwhelming sense of relief.

"Seeing those miners was the biggest lift I got all day long," Summers said.

Ameren crews arrived quickly to work on the dangerous downed electric lines. At one point there were 200 Ameren trucks on the scene.

Volunteer groups including Samaritans Purse, an evangelical relief organization, and Operation Blessing, a nonprofit humanitarian organization, came to stay in the community.

In addition to consoling those who were grieving, Operation Blessing volunteers provided meals, helped rebuild houses and cleared debris for 21 days.

"Operation Blessing was truly a blessing," Summers said. More than 2,000 volunteers showed up on the Saturday after the tornado to help.

The Harrisburg Ministerial Alliance organized a worship and prayer service at the high school for those grieving their losses. The group raised more than $6,000 for the disaster relief fund.

Although the 78-bed Harrisburg Medical Center was damaged, no one in the building was injured. It remained open and treated scores of the injured.

Felty said officials set up a staging area so medical evacuation helicopters from LifeFlight of Evansville, Ind. and Arch Air Medical Service of St. Louis could transport seriously injured people to larger hospitals.

One entity that did not shoulder a major cleanup burden – the federal government. Twice it rejected Harrisburg's request for federal disaster aid, saying the uninsured damages did not meet the required threshold.

'THAT NICE LADY... READY TO RETIRE.'"

Six people died on Feb. 29 - Jaylynn Ferrell, 22; Greg Swierk, 50; Donna Rann, 61 and her husband, Randy Rann, 64; Linda Hull, 74; and Mary Osman, 75. Two more died later - Robert Smith, 70, on March 7 and Blaine Mauney, 74, on May 31.

Six of the people who lost their lives were residents of an apartment complex on Brady Street that had been built eight years ago.

One was Donna Rann, who worked at the Shawnee National Forest Headquarters in Harrisburg for the past eight years.

"People will come in and ask, 'Where's that nice lady who wrote me a permit – the one who was getting ready to retire?'" said Wendy Cowsert a coworker. "She was like a second mom to me."

At one point, 200 Ameren trucks responded to help in the aftermath. | NATHAN HOEFERT

Debris and insulation from the tornado are snagged by a fence in a Harrisburg neighborhood. | STEVE MATZKER

There's just too much space.
That was all houses before

Rann and her husband had both received good news just days before the tornado about some health problems they were each having, Cowsert said.

But Cowsert says it was a blessing that the Ranns took their visiting grandson, Gavin, home earlier in the evening.

Another Brady Street resident, Jaylynn Ferrell, was the youngest person to die. She was 22 and had just earned her nursing degree.

Miki Pavelonis works with Jaylynn's grandmother, Ann Ferrell, at State Rep. Brandon Phelps' office.

"Jaylynn was her life," Pavelonis said of Ann. "Jaylynn was as sweet as they come. She had just finished her RN degree and had her whole life ahead of her."

The last person to die was Blaine Mauney, the man found in the bathtub. He died at his son's house May 31.

Roy Mauney's wife, Melissa, said their sons, Brice, 16, and Ethan, 11, work with them almost every day as they rebuild the house that now only Rebecca will occupy.

"It's really important to get my mother back in her house," Roy Mauney said.

Melissa worried that while her mother-in-law has recovered from her physical injuries, she may not get over losing her husband of more than 40 years.

She looked down the hill behind her mother-in-law's property and added, "There's just too much space. That was all houses before."

Bob Pavelonis (left) and Mark Whitler inspect damage to the Pavelonis' home on Sullivan Street, just hours after the tornado hit. Whitler, a family friend, had installed the cabinetry in the home in 2010. Miki Pavelonis said she and her husband Bob were awakened by the family dogs moments before the tornado hit. "We could have been killed," she said. | NICOLE HESTER

Most residents whose homes were in the path of the deadly tornado lost irreplaceable treasures that day, such as family photos and a lifetime of collected memorabilia. Recovered photos were initially displayed in the library for residents to identify, according to Sherry Hinant, genealogy librarian. Unclaimed photos were later boxed and moved to the offices of the Harrisburg Daily Register. | PAT SUTPHIN

Loeva Raymer, 88, a retired school teacher, stands amid her belongings in the front yard of her home on Roosevelt Street.
| JON-ERIK BRADFORD

Volunteers quickly joined together to clear debris from Dream Baskets Gifts and Cafe, which has since been reopened. | JESSICA TEZAK

14

Ethan Mauney, 11, of Harrisburg, stands on the front porch where a home used to stand in Harrisburg. Ethan said his grandparents were in the hospital for injuries sustained from the storm. His grandfather, Blaine Mauney, died from his injuries May 31. | ISAAC SMITH

Katie Turner hauls off a piece of insulation as she helps in the cleanup efforts at the home of her grandparents Charles and Diana Turner. | JESSICA TEZAK

Amanda Emerson holds her daughter, Khloe Humphrey, on her porch in Harrisburg. Emerson's husband, Richard Emerson, said the inside of the house was undamaged, but it shook as the storm moved through the area. | ISAAC SMITH

Aruniti Manawa stands near her neighbors' Harrisburg home as she waits for her family to gather some belongings from their damaged home. Manawa's father, Dr. Brahm Jyot, had moved his family to Harrisburg from Chicago eight months earlier. | STEVE MATZKER

The tornado destroyed St. Joseph's Catholic Church in Ridgway. All that remained of the 110-year-old gothic style church was the entrance door, altar, and tabernacle. | ISAAC SMITH

The tornado that leveled St. Joseph's Catholic Church hit Ridgway at 5:10 a.m., injuring 12 people and damaging 140 homes and businesses in that community. | CHRIS ZOELLER

Ruth Ann Wallace, of Harrisburg, stands in her daughter's kitchen after the tornado tore the roof off the house. Her daughter, Lisa Thomas had lived in the house for 25 years. | JESSICA TEZAK

A man peers through the window of one of the more than 200 damaged homes in Harrisburg. About 25 businesses were also damaged or destroyed by the tornado. | NICOLE HESTER

Steve McDonald stands upon the remains of a destroyed home. The 275-yard-wide path of destruction left several areas unscathed while others nearby were destroyed. | PAT SUTPHIN

Volunteers from religious groups, schools, and civic organizations streamed into Harrisburg during the days following the storm. Harrisburg Fire Chief Bill Summers praised their efforts, saying, "We didn't have people wanting glory. We had workers." | JAMIE BIRCHFIELD

Elizabeth Thomas, of Indiana, who was visiting her boyfriend, Dustin Patterson, at the Brady Street apartments, was hit in the face by flying debris while being thrown nearly half a block by the tornado. | ERIC GINNARD

Elizabeth Thomas talks on her cell phone while her boyfriend, Dustin Patterson ,of Harrisburg, observes the damage to his father's truck and sheds. Thomas and Patterson sustained minor injuries from being tossed by the tornado's 185-mph winds. | DANIELLE MCGREW

(From left to right) Eldorado firefighters Cody Mitchell, Patrick Mings, and Derek McKinnies patrol the streets of the Garden Heights section of Harrisburg the morning of the storm. | LYNNETTE OOSTMEYER

Hurst Fire Captain Colton Woolsey and another Hurst firefighter help move belongings from the wreckage. They were among 14 departments that responded to assist Harrisburg as part of the mutual aid box alarm system, known as MABAS. More than 1,300 departments in Illinois, Wisconsin, Indiana and Missouri provide assistance to each other using pre-determined "box cards" outlining what specific equipment is needed to respond to various emergencies. | SAMANTHA VAUGHN

Employees from Peabody Energy Company's Willow Lake, Cottage Grove, Gateway and Wildcat Hills mines responded immediately to the disaster in Harrisburg. "They're already trained in rescue operations so they were a great help," said Allan Ninness, director of the Saline County Emergency Management Agency. | LYNNETTE OOSTMEYER

The Cash Store, Hibbett's Sports and Gamestop were among the businesses destroyed by the early morning tornado that hit a strip mall on the south side of town. | JAMIE BIRCHFIELD

Wayne Poteet, 38, stands next to his semi-trailer that was flipped on its side from the force of the tornado. Poteet had made an early morning delivery to a furniture store and had parked his truck in the Wal-Mart parking lot to get some rest. | JAMIE BIRCHFIELD

Dena McDonald stands in the wreckage of her mother's Brady Street home. McDonald's mother, Mary Osman, was one of the eight people who died as a result of the tornado. | SAMANTHA VAUGHN

Even during the grim days following the disaster, some of the tornado's victims maintained a sense of humor. Sharon Murray's house was damaged, but that didn't keep her granddaughter, Lindsey Murray, 15 from advertising the house "for sale" and posting a notice that a prosthetic leg had been found amid the rubble. | TIFFANY BLANCHETTE

Cindy Winters looks for salvageable items among the wreckage of a neighbor's home in the Dorrisville neighborhood. Kerry Jones, whose house on Largent Street was also damaged, described the sound he heard as the tornado hit the area. "It sounded like four jet engines and 30 people beating with ball bats on the side of our house," he said. | ERIC GINNARD

Gale Milligan looks over some of the damage left by the Leap Day tornado. Milligan's business, Energy Mart, was destroyed in the tornado, but he and his son Joe began cleaning up immediately after. | JON-ERIK BRADFORD

Volunteer workers clear debris from the tornado that Harrisburg Mayor Eric Gregg described as being "three or four football fields wide." | LYNNETTE OOSTMEYER

Jennifer Osman stifles a sob as she looks at a picture she and her fiancé, Brad Reed, found while searching through the rubble of her grandmother, Mary Osman's, home. Mary Osman died in the storm. | PAT SUTPHIN

The tornado tore away three walls of Keith Huke's house at the corner of Birch and Water Street. Huke was asleep in the bed when the storm struck but he was not injured. | LYNNETTE OOSTMEYER

Steve Riley, who helped his grandmother, Utha Angelly, after her house was destroyed, looks across her yard at the contents of her living room. | DANIELLE MCGREW

Joe Milligan pulls a carving nicknamed "Ol' Lucky" made by a friend from the rubble of his father's business, Energy Mart, a fireplace and gas log shop. | NICOLE HESTER

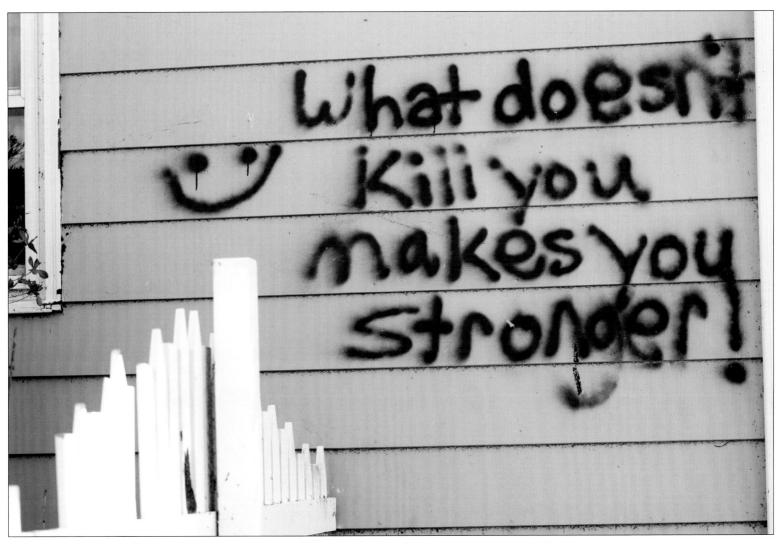

Some Harrisburg residents dealt with the devastation through humor. | CHRIS ZOELLER

Keith Huke, of Harrisburg, looks at debris in the living room of his house on Water Street. "The main items I want to find are my medications, my calico cat and my arrowhead collection, which are all very important to me," he said. Huke did find his cat. | LYNNETTE OOSTMEYER

Harrisburg residents used spray paint to alert friends they were safe. Messages such as this appeared throughout the devastated areas, said William "Taz" Karns, a Saline County Emergency Management Agency worker. "There were signs everywhere," he said. | NICOLE HESTER

Volunteers raise the side of one of the houses destroyed by the tornado. Joy Emery, whose nearby home was also damaged during the tornado, said she and her husband couldn't have made it to their basement in time even if they had tried. She said she was awakened by the sound of two carports being blown into their house. "The tornado came so quickly," she said. "It was here and gone in a flash." | NICOLE HESTER

Julie Shaw and Vince Stevers help Marilyn Shimkus, left, gather some of her belongings in plastic bags after the tornado severely damaged her home. | LYNNETTE OOSTMEYER

Barb Trammel helps salvage items from the living room of her friends' home on Sullivan Street on the southside of Harrisburg. | JESSICA TEZAK

Terry Turpin, of Troy, Mo., sweeps debris off his friend's porch Feb. 29. Turpin said he came to help out as soon as he heard the news. | STEVE MATZKER

Jane Buti, of Terre Haute, Ind., was visiting her longtime friend, Utha Angelly, at her home on Largent Street. Buti and Angelly were not seriously injured despite the extensive damage to Angelly's house. | ERIC GINNARD

Utha Angelly, a resident of Harrisburg, recounts the moments after the tornado hit her home. Angelly was asleep in her bed when the roof crashed onto her. She yelled for help until her neighbor, Ronald Patterson, removed the debris and rescued her and her friend. "It was like waking up in a nightmare," Angelly said. | DANIELLE MCGREW

Scarlett Winters walks with Dillon Parker along the tornado's path of destruction on Largent Street in Harrisburg.
| NATHAN HOEFERT

Eddie Brooks, of Harrisburg, looks through the car of his friend, Brandon Culkin, Wednesday for Culkin's lost helmet. Brooks said Culkin, a storm spotter, was in the car when the storm hit but said he was not seriously injured. | NICOLE HESTER

Village of Ridgway employee Tom Ozee directs trucks filled with storm debris toward a burn pile Saturday March 3 outside Ridgway Park. City employees and volunteers began burning and consolidating storm debris Saturday morning. | ISAAC SMITH

A chair and a flowerpot are among the salvageable belongings from a house damaged by the capricious tornado. Some houses in its path remained relatively unscathed, while others were destroyed. | SARAH GARDNER

Undamaged furniture is salvaged from the wreckage of a house. | ERIC GINNARD

Melanie Reed, of Harrisburg, distributes supplies to help with the cleanup of the tornado's aftermath. | NATHAN HOEFERT

Terry Winters, Jr. and Bobby Patterson, Jr. set headstones upright in a cemetery on the southwest side of Harrisburg. | ERIC GINNARD

Eli and Molly Shires were two of the many young volunteers who helped carry relief supplies into the First Baptist Church in Harrisburg. The church provided a headquarters for Red Cross Disaster Services and shelter for victims displaced by the storm. | NATHAN HOEFERT

Matt Winkleman and Steve Williams, both of Harrisburg, load water onto a truck Wednesday outside the First Baptist Church of Harrisburg. | NATHAN HOEFERT

Reporters and photographers from across the country gathered to hear Harrisburg Mayor Eric Gregg and Illinois Governor Pat Quinn speak at the afternoon press conference Feb. 29. | JESSICA TEZAK

Harrisburg mayor Eric Gregg (left), Lt. Gov. Sheila Simon (middle) and Governor Pat Quinn appeared at a press conference Feb. 29 as the governor declared a disaster area, making it eligible for funding to rebuild the devastated areas of the city. | JESSICA TEZAK

Jaime Reynolds, 13, compresses debris in a bucket at a baseball field in Ridgway the day after the tornado. "I play in this field everyday and this is my town and I don't want to see it this way," she said. "It is just really sad." | SAMANTHA VAUGHN

Volunteers from nearby communities immediately arrived to clear debris. In the days following the tornado, emergency workers and others from hundreds of miles away came to offer assistance. | ERIC GINNARD

Harrison Milligan, 6, cradles the American flag as he looks at the carnage left by the tornado. Harrison's grandfather's business, Energy Mart, was demolished during the storm. | ALEXA ROGALS

Donna Rice, of Carrier Mills, holds her 4-year-old grandson, D.J. Rice. Donna Rice came to help her brother, Ron Patterson, clean up his home on Largent Street. | ERIC GINNARD

The American flag flew at the funerals of the six Harrisburg residents who lost their lives Feb. 29. | DANIELLE MCGREW

Members of the Osman family grieve at the community worship service held at the Harrisburg High School March 4. Their family matriarch, Mary Osman, 75, was laid to rest March 3. | PAT SUTPHIN

Serving the community since 1945.

God is our refuge and strength, an ever-present help in trouble.
Psalm 46:1

HMC Medical Staff Answers The Call During a Tragic Tornado

HMC Storm Recovery | 02.29.12

While February 29th is always a notable day - after all it only comes around every four years - this specific day in 2012 is one the citizens of Harrisburg and the surrounding region will never forget. Whether you came face-to-face with the tornado, or volunteered during the aftermath - the storm, the damage and the shock felt in its wake left a huge impression on all of us.

Harrisburg Medical Center, of course, plays an active role in our community's emergency response system, working in concert with EMS and other partners to provide the people of our region with a wide array of emergency services during this and any other disasters. Our staff is well trained in disaster preparedness and the systems we have in place at HMC ensure our ability to respond and serve at a moment's notice.

This preparedness and training was evident during the February 29th storm. We are proud that our ability allowed us to ensure the following:

- The Emergency Department and Supporting Departments Never Closed
- All Inpatients (42) Were Evacuated with No Injuries
- Emergency Department Staff Treated 50 Tornado Victims
- HMC Provided Countless Meals and Shelter to Victims and Volunteers
- Buildings were Sealed and Damaged Areas Quarantined by the Evening of February 29th
- 50% of Inpatient Beds Re-opened April 6th
- Cardiac Rehab, Cardiac Stress Testing & Nuclear Medicine Reopened April 16th

The section of hospital that was most heavily damaged will have to remain closed for over one year. It is slated to re-open June 2013.

100 Dr. Warren Tuttle Drive, Harrisburg
618.253.7671 | www.HarrisburgMC.com

Credits

Student Photographers

Jamie Birchfield
Tiffany Blanchette
Jon-Erik Bradford
Sarah Gardner
Eric Ginnard
Nicole Hester
Nathan Hoefert
Steve Matzker
Danielle McGrew
Lynnette Oostmeyer
Alexa Rogals
Isaac Smith
Patrick Sutphin
Jessica Tezak
Samantha Vaughn
Chris Zoeller

Front Cover Photo: Les Wallace walks down Water Street soon after the tornado struck. Wallace said the duplex he was living in was completely destroyed. "I don't know how I survived," he said. | STEVE MATZKER

Back Cover Photo: People from across the region gathered on East Sloan Street to support those affected by the tornado. | LYNNETTE OOSTMEYER

Special Thanks

Residents of Harrisburg and Ridgway
The Daily Egyptian Staff
SIUC Chancellor Rita H. Cheng
Dean Gary Kolb, College of Mass Communication and Media Arts
The Howard R. Long Opportunity Fund established by SIU alumna Judith Roales

Photojournalism Faculty
Mark Dolan
Phillip Greer

Copy Editor
Sharon Wittke

Photo Editor
Steve Matzker

Design Editor
Lauren Leone

Advertising Coordinators
Erin Morris
Ann-Marie Nichols
Alex Scates
Matthew Weidenbenner

Journalism Faculty
William Freivogel
William Recktenwald

Jon-Erik Bradford, a SIU photojournalism student, helps Joe Milligan fold a flag found tangled in a tree at his father's store, Energy Mart, that was destroyed in the tornado. Bradford is an 8-year veteran of the U.S. Army. Harrison Milligan, 6, stands behind his father. | NICOLE HESTER

PHOTO BY PAT SUTPHIN

Jaylynn Ferrell
Linda Hull
Blaine Mauney
Mary Osman
Donna Rann
Randy Rann
Robert Smith
Greg Swierk

Epilogue

*The tornado that ripped into Harrisburg Feb. 29, 2012
at 4:56 a.m. tore through the heart of the city before
battering Ridgway, 15 miles away.*

*People in both communities immediately responded
to rescue those trapped beneath the wreckage. They
tended to the injured and helped their neighbors
salvage precious belongings.*

*Shortly after the devastated areas were secured,
thousands of volunteers came to aid in the clean-up
efforts, hauling away endless truckloads of rubble.*

*But the sounds of debris disposal would soon be
replaced with the sounds of hammers and saws as the
two towns began to repair and rebuild.*

*Bright blue tarps covering damaged homes gave
way to new roofs. The frames of new houses sprouted
like spring flowers as workers, braving record high
temperatures, labored tirelessly.*

*While those minutes before dawn were the worst
Harrisburg and Ridgway ever experienced, the hours,
weeks and months after the tornado were their finest.*

A robin perches on debris left by the tornado in front of the
siren that alerted the community to the approaching danger.
| NICOLE HESTER